CONTENTS

INTRODUCTION

Squash, or to give the game its full title, squash rackets, is a popular sport. It is competitive and increases fitness; it is also fun and a great social activity. Most beginner players find it is an easy sport to learn.

IMPROVING SQUASH

Whether you are a beginner or a more experienced squash player, guidance and advice are essential to becoming better at the sport and to getting more fun from the game. The best form of guidance is individual coaching from a qualified coach, but this book will provide you with the essentials to help you to the next level, or if you are lucky enough to receive regular training, it will reinforce the skills you learn during coaching sessions.

The advice on play in this book was written by the late Sam Jagger, who coached squash at Lancing College for 27 years, with contributions from the Performance Coaching Team at England Squash.

This book assumes players are right-handed. Left-handed players should reverse these instructions.

SCORING

The scoring described in this book is the standard (or International) system, in which games are up to 9 points and points can only be scored when you are serving hand-in (serving to start the rally). This system is used in the women's professional game. The men's professional game uses the 'point-a-rally' (PAR) system, where games are up to 11 points and every point is scored, i.e. a player receiving serve (hand-out) wins a point as well as the service when the server (hand-in) serves a fault or loses a rally (see pages 10 and 13).

Notice how carefully these two top players are watching the ball.

Riverbank
Park Plaza
Brit
Insurance

THE GAME

Squash is usually played between two players, but doubles matches are also possible for more experienced players (see page 42). It is a racket and ball game, played on an enclosed court. It is different to racketball, which is featured on pages 54–55.

THE BASICS

At the start of a squash game between two players the ball is served by one player, from a service box, on to the front wall above the cut line. On its rebound, the serve must fall into the opposite back quarter of the court bounded by the half-court line and the short line (see the diagram opposite).

The server is known as 'hand-in' and the receiver as 'hand-out'. Following the serve, hand-out may either volley the ball or hit the ball after it has bounced once on the floor. In either case, he or she plays the ball to the front wall either directly or off a side or back wall.

A service return is fair or 'good' if the ball:

- remains within the boundaries of the court
- hits the front wall above the tin before it touches the floor
- does not bounce on the floor more than once before it is returned.

The server receives and returns the ball, and a rally continues in this alternating way. Play continues until a player fails to make a good return, when his or her opponent scores a point (if hand-in) or takes over the service (if hand-out).

MATCH OFFICIALS

A marker and referee adjudicate in organised matches. The referee is in overall control and makes all decisions covering lets, the award of points, and appeals against calls of the marker by either player. Where there is only one official, he or she must act as marker and referee.

The dimensions of a squash court.

THE COURT

Squash courts have a number of standard features.

- The walls of a squash court are traditionally white or near white. The use of colour in squash courts is permitted subject to the relevant World Squash Federation (WSF) guidelines.
- The size of the court is standard and all floor and wall dimensions are measured from the junction of the floor and walls.
- Lines are painted red and are 50mm wide, whether on the floor or walls of the court.
- The 'tin' consists of a plywood or metal sheet extending right across the front wall.
- A strip of wood above the tin is known as the board and is painted red.

In squash, only the server can score points.

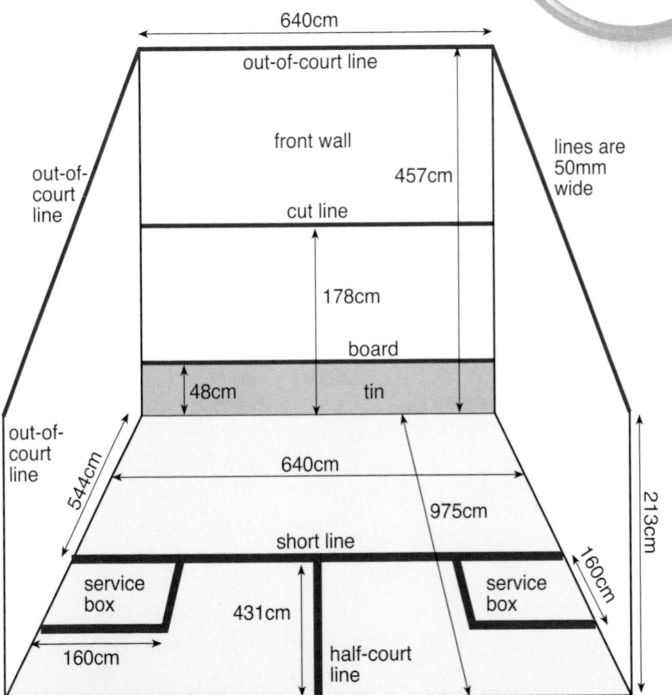

EQUIPMENT

It is important to start out with the correct equipment, especially footwear. A suitable squash racket can usually be chosen by 'feel', so try and play with a number of different rackets to decide which weight and design is most comfortable. A coach at your local club will be able to advise you.

CLOTHING

As with other sports, squash clothing incorporates the latest technical developments. You should wear clothes that are comfortable and do not cause your body to overheat. The latest fitted microfibre shirts are designed for ease of movement and comfort, as well as for looking good on court.

- The standard clothing for men is shorts, white squash shoes with soles that do not mark the floor, and a short-sleeved shirt.
- Women normally wear a fitted vest or shirt with a short skirt or shorts, or a short dress.

THE RACKET

Make sure the racket that you select incorporates the following features:

- the head and shaft are made of graphite
- the grip is made of leather, and overgrips are used to help absorb perspiration
- the racket is strung with techni-fibre, nylon or a similar material
- there may be some 'whip' in the shaft
- the maximum weight is not more than 255g
- the maximum strung area is not more than 500cm^2.

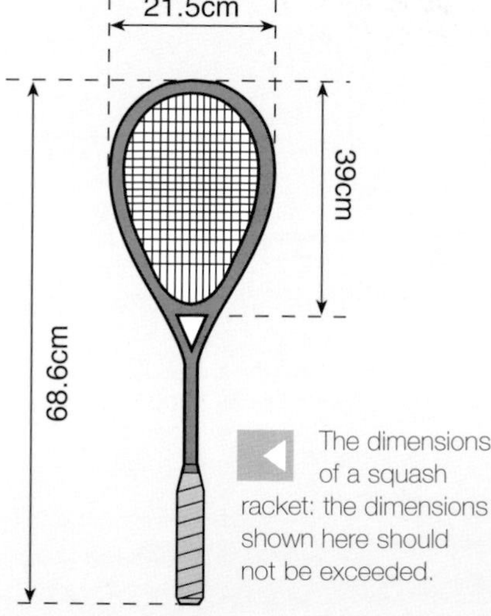

The dimensions of a squash racket: the dimensions shown here should not be exceeded.

THE BALL

Squash balls are made of rubber and are small and round with an even matt surface and finish.

- Balls come in two speeds to suit the ability of the player and/or the temperature of the court.
- Ball speeds are indicated by coloured dots: single yellow dot (very slow 'Competition' ball, used by most regular players); and double yellow dot (extra super slow 'Pro' ball, used only in the professional game).

Balls should weigh 24g. Those that meet the specifications of the WSF can be identified by the WSF or National Association logo.

A light blue 'Max' ball, 12 per cent larger than the standard size is designed for beginners. 'Improvers' can use a black 'Progress' ball that is 6 per cent larger than standard.

IN THE KIT BAG

Items you will need for training sessions or competitions:

- spare balls
- sports bag or holdall
- tracksuit
- drink bottle
- light snacks
- change of shirt and socks
- spare racket grip
- two towels
- eye protection, i.e. glasses that meet national safety standards for squash:
  GB – BS79301
  USA – ASTMG803
  Canada – CSAP400
  Australia – A/N24066.

It is compulsory for all players aged 18 and under to wear eye protection in national and international competition.

The name 'squash' comes from the 'squashable' ball used in the game.

SERVICE

The right to serve first is decided by the spin of a racket, and the server may serve from either service box. A number of rules determine whether a serve is fair or foul. When a fault is served, the right to serve is lost. Otherwise, play continues until the end of the rally.

PATTERN OF PLAY

A rally between players 'X' and 'Y' usually develops as follows:

- player X wins the spin of the racket and serves
- player Y returns the ball and from then it is struck alternately until X either wins a point or loses the service
- X continues to score points as long as he or she continues to win rallies while serving
- if X puts the ball out of court, into the tin or board, serves a fault or is beaten by Y's return, Y becomes the server
- this pattern continues throughout the match.

For the initial service of each game or 'hand', the server may serve from either box. Points are scored by hand-in when his or her opponent fails to make a good return. After scoring a point, hand-in must serve from the other box, alternating service from each box for as long as he or she is hand-in.

SERVICE

There are a few simple rules that need to be followed when serving.

- Stand with one foot or both feet touching the floor completely within the service box.
- Throw the ball into the air.
- Serve the ball on to the front wall above the service line so that on its return, unless volleyed, it would fall on the floor in the quarter court nearest the back wall and opposite to the service box from which the service has been delivered.

FOOT FAULTS

In each of these cases, the server is at fault and loses the service.

- The server must have at least one foot in contact with the floor, within the service box, at the moment of striking the ball.
- No part of the qualifying foot may be touching a line, the wall or the floor outside the box, though the other foot may be anywhere inside or outside the box.

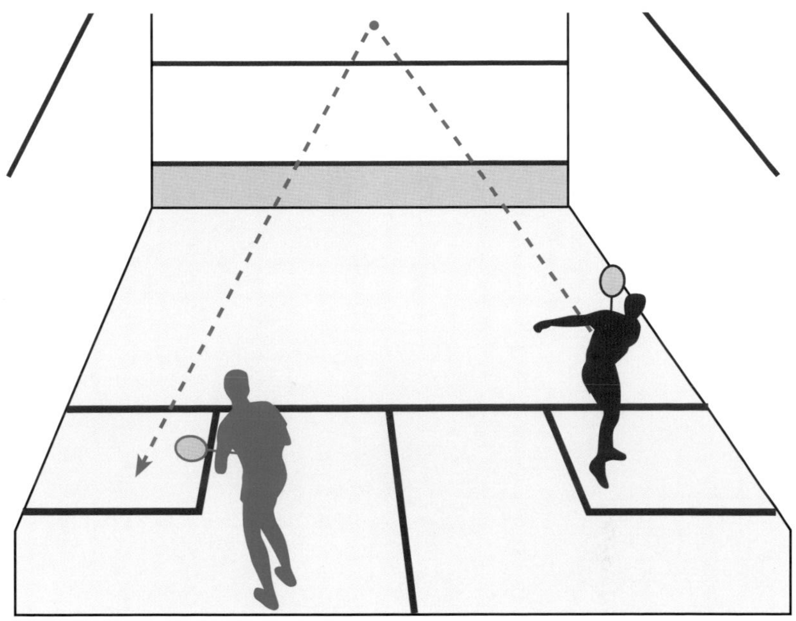

The service: if hand-in (the red player) serves from the right-hand service box, he or she may take up the position shown here, ready to deliver a forehand service. A backhand stroke may also be used from this service box. A service from the left-hand box may also be served either forehand or backhand.

SERVING FROM THE WRONG BOX

- If hand-in serves from the wrong box and the opponent takes the service, there is no penalty and the service counts as if it had been made from the correct box.
- An opponent may ask for the service to be re-taken from the correct box, provided he or she has not returned or attempted to return the service.

If you serve well you start the rally in control. Always try to volley an opponent's service.

A rally begins with a forehand or backhand serve.

OTHER SERVICE FAULTS

In each of the following cases, the server is at fault and loses the service.

- The ball is served to the front wall on or below the service line.
- The ball first touches the floor on the half-court line or in the half court from which the service is delivered.
- The ball first touches the floor on or in front of the short line, i.e. it drops short of the service court.
- The server fails to hit the ball correctly (termed 'not up').
- The server serves the ball out of court.
- The ball strikes another wall before the front wall.
- The ball touches the server, their clothing or racket before an attempt to return is made.

CONTINUING PLAY

After a good service has been delivered, play continues. A return of service is good if the ball, before it has bounced twice on the floor, is returned by the striker either directly into the front wall above the tin, or on to the side wall then the front wall, without touching the floor or any part of the striker's body or clothing.

WINNING THE RALLY

A player wins the rally in the following cases:

- his or her opponent who is hand-in serves a fault or loses the rally
- the opponent fails to make a good return of the ball in play
- the ball touches the striker's opponent or anything he or she wears or carries, except in cases of obstruction (see page 16–17).

Play continues with alternating return shots.

Hand-in scores a point if he or she wins the rally. Hand-out gains the service if he or she wins the rally.

SCORING

Matches are controlled by the officials, who keep score and adjudicate on all appeals. The officials must judge all shots to be fair or unfair, and will call for a let (see page 16–17) to be played in the event of obstruction.

DURATION OF A MATCH

A match consists of the best of five games, and each game is 9-up. The first player to score nine points wins the game, except in the following situation.

- If the score is called 8-all for the first time, before the next service is delivered, hand-out may choose to set the game to two. In this case, the first player to score two points wins the game. The two points do not have to be scored consecutively.
- Hand-out must clearly indicate his or her choice to the marker, if any, and to the opponent, by saying either 'Set one' or 'Set two'. The score does not go beyond ten. Thus, in the case of 'Set one', one player will win the game 9-8. In the case of 'Set two', one player will win 10-9 or 10-8.

KEEPING SCORE

- An organised game is controlled by the marker, who calls the play and score. The server's score is called first.
- If during play the marker calls 'Not up', 'Out' or 'Down', the rally must stop.
- If the marker's decision is altered on appeal, a 'let' is allowed, unless the referee decides that the marker has called 'Not up', 'Out' or 'Down' to a certain winning shot that was fair. In this case, the referee may award the stroke accordingly.

Obstructing another player is not allowed.

APPEALS TO THE REFEREE

- Hand-in may appeal against the marker's call of 'Fault', 'Foot-fault', 'Out', 'Down' or 'Not up'.
- Hand-out may appeal against the marker's failure to make any of these calls. In this case he or she should play the ball and appeal only if the rally is lost.

All appeals are directed to the referee. His or her decision is final.

LETS

A let is an undecided rally. The rally does not count and the server serves again from the same box.

WSF Rule 13

A let may be allowed if the ball in play touches any article lying on the floor, or if the striker refrains from hitting the ball owing to a reasonable fear of injuring the opponent. A let must also be allowed if the receiver is not ready and does not attempt to return the service, or if the ball breaks during play.

PLAYING FAIR

- A player must do all he or she can to give their opponent a clear and fair view of the ball in play and room to play a shot.
- Try to practise your movement and shot accuracy; this will help prevent unnecessary obstruction on court.

WSF Rule 12

Interference – let or stroke ?

When it is his or her turn to play the ball, a player is entitled to freedom from interference by the opponent.

To avoid interference, the opponent must try to provide the player with unobstructed direct access to the ball, a fair view of the ball, space to complete a swing at the ball and freedom to play the ball directly to any part of the front wall.

When play has stopped as a result of interference the general guidelines are:

- the player is entitled to a let if he or she could have returned the ball and the opponent has made every effort to avoid interference
- the player is not entitled to a let if he or she could not have returned the ball or accepts the interference and plays on
- the player is entitled to a stroke if the opponent did not make every effort to avoid interference, or if the player would have a hit a winning return.

Squash is an attacking, dynamic game, which requires a good level of fitness.

OTHER EXAMPLES OF LETS V. STROKES

If a fair ball, after hitting the front wall and before being played again, touches a player or anything he or she wears or carries before touching the floor twice, the touched player loses the rally.

A player wins the stroke when his or her opponent fails to make a good return. In this case, the blue player loses the rally.

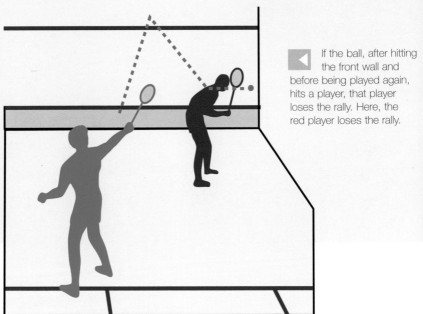

If the ball, after hitting the front wall and before being played again, hits a player, that player loses the rally. Here, the red player loses the rally.

If a ball is struck as a good return and it hits the striker's opponent before it reaches the front wall, it is a stroke to the striker if the ball would have reached the front wall directly – unless the striker had 'turned' on the ball, or has already played and missed.

A fair return that would have hit the front wall but hits an opponent first is awarded to the striker. In this case, the red player loses the rally.

If a ball is struck as a good return and hits the opponent on its way to either side wall, it is a let. Similarly, if a good return has already hit the side wall on its way to the front wall it is also a let, unless a winning shot has been intercepted, in which case a stroke is awarded.

The ball hits the opponent on its way to the side wall. In this case, a let is played.

If a ball strikes an opponent but would not have made a good return, the striker loses the stroke.

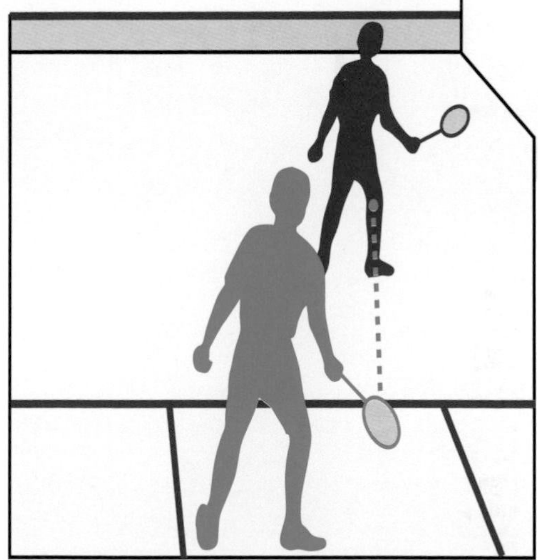

In this case, the ball would not have hit the front wall so the blue player loses the stroke.

BASIC STROKES

Basic forehand and backhand strokes incorporate a preparation, swing and follow-through – work on getting these right. Watch top players in action to see how they produce accurate and consistent strokes. They have great ball control through good technique.

GRIP

Before you can start to improve your basic strokes, make sure that you are happy with your grip. The correct grip is the same for both forehand and backhand strokes.

- First 'shake hands' with the handle. Make sure there is a slight gap between forefinger and second finger.
- Form a 'V' between the thumb and forefinger, presenting the racket with an open face as shown in the photo below.

A good striking technique is as important in squash as it is in golf or tennis.

- Do not grip the racket tightly. Your whole body should be balanced and relaxed when you are in a position to strike the ball. It is the fingers that hold the racket, not the palm of your hand.
- Squeeze your grip when you strike the ball, then relax it in the follow-through.
- Try to maintain 'soft hands' to develop touch and feel in your game.

STRIKING THE BALL

Try to form an effective hitting technique as early as possible. This helps with both accuracy and power.

- The most important reason for establishing a proper striking technique is accuracy, i.e. to control the racket face, and direction and pace of the ball.
- A consistent backswing, downswing and follow-through on both sides of the court will also minimise the chances of hitting your opponent with the racket.

FOREHAND AND BACKHAND

The first strokes you will practise are likely to be drives to the back of the court. The following section describes the backswing, making contact with the ball and following through. Practise these elements to improve the control, accuracy and safety of all your forehand and backhand play.

Backswing

The backswing is the preparation of the stroke. The height of backswing will vary depending on the type of shot that you wish to play.

- Always take the racket out in the first instance, then upwards from the body to create space between elbow and body throughout the backswing. Make sure the racket head is higher than the wrist at the top of the backswing.
- Always arrive in position to play the ball with the backswing ready. If you get to the ball with the racket head not ready, there is no time to prepare the backswing and you will be late on the shot.
- The backswing should always be prepared with the elbow slightly bent and the racket head pushed upwards.

The wrist should maintain control of the racket head at all times and be quite firm but must not be cocked.

Notice the player's wrist position in this forehand stroke.

DIFFERENT GRIPS

Some players have developed their own grip variations. A grip is correct provided it:

- **has an open face**
- **is comfortable**
- **allows control of direction of the ball**
- **allows the full range of forehand and backhand stokes to be played successfully.**

The strike...

If you wish to play the straight drive – one of the most common shots – either forehand or backhand side, this is the correct technique to practise.

- The racket head is delivered in a smooth throwing action with the body stable and the elbow fully extended on impact.
- Once again, the racket face should be open on contact.

...and finish

The final phase of the stroke is the follow-through. For a right-handed player, the racket head should finish towards the left shoulder (forehand) or right shoulder (backhand). After contact and follow-through there is a natural recoil action to return the racket back to start position.

PRO POWER

- Top-class players obtain their control and power from great timing, early and effective preparation, and the transfer of weight from the back to the front foot, then on to the ball, on impact. They are balanced throughout their movement and striking.
- Good squash players never generate power from pure physical strength.

In all strokes, follow-through upwards rather than outwards. The latter can be dangerous to an opponent, and risks penalty at advanced competitive level.

Notice how well balanced this player is before striking the ball.

Slazenger
DUN

POSITIONS FOR STRIKING THE BALL

Becoming a better squash player is partly about improving your ability to select the best type of stroke according to your position and the position of the ball. Be aware of the range of options that you have – you can strike from in front of or behind the ball, taking the ball early or late. You also have options for the type of stroke at the serve and service return – learn to vary your play.

SHOT POSITIONING

Good shot positioning refers to the position you take up before you strike the ball.

There are three positions from which you can take the ball in relation to your leading foot (i.e. the left foot on the right-hand side of the court and the right foot on the left-hand side of the court – this is easily remembered as the foot nearer the front wall when facing the nearer side wall).

1. **In front of the leading foot**
   This position makes it easier to strike the ball from one side of the court to the other, i.e. to play a cross-drive, cross-lob or cross-drop shot.

2. **In line with the leading foot**
   This is a very important position as it is used to hit the ball straight down the side walls, i.e. a straight drive from the front or back, straight volley or straight drop shot.

3. **Behind the leading foot – 'taking the ball late'**
   This position is usually used when you need to hit the side walls before the front wall, i.e. a 'boast' (see page 26) out of the back corners, or short angled shots at the front of the court. This position is used to help disguise shots.

A good rally is one where you manage to play every shot away from your opponent.

GOOD SHOT TIMING

There are three basic ways to strike the ball as it bounces off the floor.

1. **On the rise or early**
   This allows you to speed up the game by moving on to the ball and taking it early, therefore hurrying your opponent.
2. **At the top of the bounce**
   This is the most common point to hit the ball as it is at its slowest and easiest to hit. Do not 'crowd' the ball.
3. **On the fall or late**
   This is used out of necessity if you are late on the shot. It is also a way of delaying your shot so that your opponent commits to one shot then has to change direction to cover another shot.

Taking the ball early is a good way of speeding up the game and pressurising your opponent's movement. This principle is crucial in the professional game.

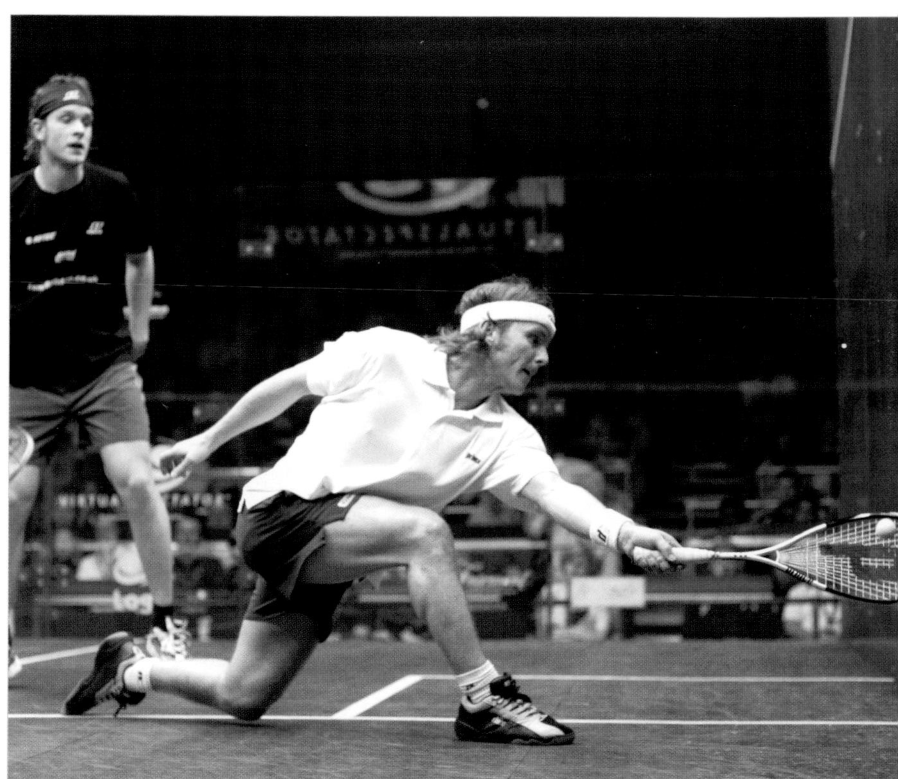

TAKING THE BALL OFF THE BACK WALL

When taking the ball off the back wall, position your body to face one of two positions:

- the side wall
- the corner.

With your racket prepared to strike the ball, remember to keep a comfortable distance away from both the side and back walls to allow space to make your swing.

The two most common returns for balls coming off the back wall are:

- A straight or cross-court return to a length. If possible, these are the best returns to make and are governed by the degree of rebound that the ball makes off the back wall. It is important to play out of back corners with control.
- A boast. This is a common return from the back corners, and is particularly useful for beginners. It is used if you feel you cannot return the ball straight. The technique is to hit under the ball, lifting it upwards on to the side wall, making an angle that will carry the ball from the side wall on to the front wall in the opposite front corner.

Do not try to play the straight return down the side wall if there is any danger of hitting the back wall with your racket as you play the shot.

A player need never be beaten, except by the ball that drops dead or clings to the back wall.

OPTIONS

There are a number of shot options with a ball that bounces off the back wall.

- A ball that hits the back wall fairly hard or high and rebounds well clear of both the side and back wall may give an opening for a wider range of shots, such as the drop shot to either front corner.
- It is not always necessary to be on the defensive when your opponent's shot goes to the back of the court. Try to keep your attacking options open.
- Your choice of shot always depends on where your opponent's ball lands in the back corners and where your opponent is.

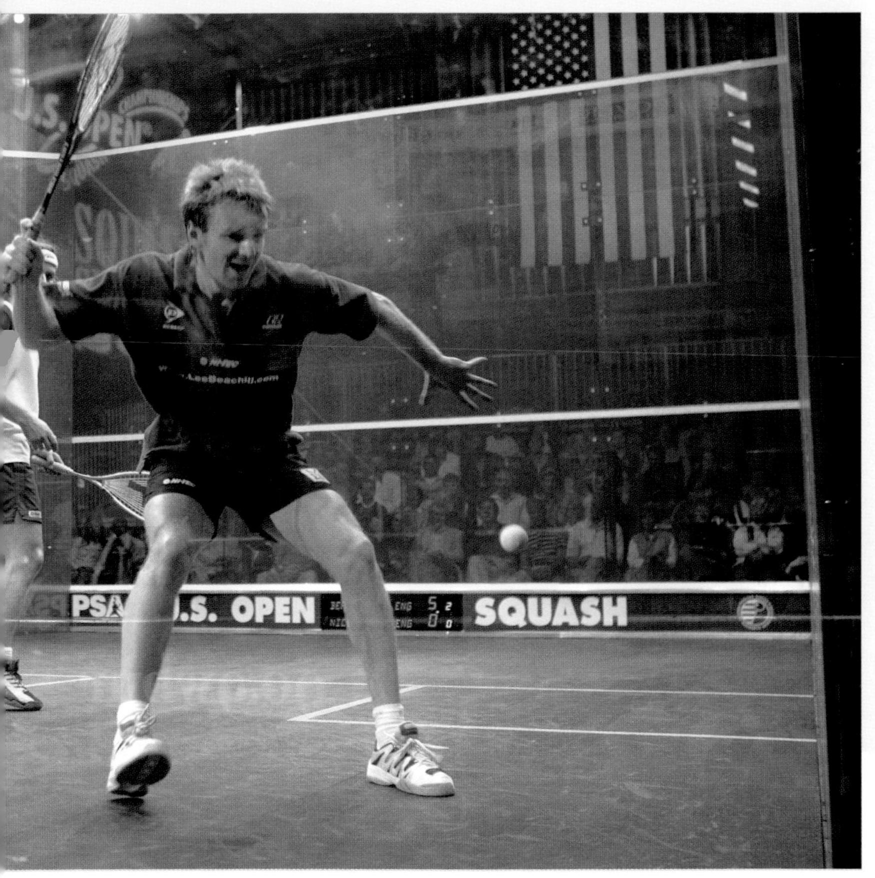

SERVICE STROKE

A lob is the best service option, so long as the height of the court roof allows.

- It should be played from the front of the service box and you should hit underneath the ball, keeping follow-through high, towards a target area near to the out-of-court line on the front wall.
- The ball should continue upwards and strike the further side wall, behind the service box. It should bounce on the floor before striking the back wall. Remember a high, soft, floating serve should ideally 'die' in the back corners.

Try to use different types of serve, both hard and soft, to mix your game up.

BACKHAND SERVE

An alternative serve from the right-hand service box is the backhand serve.

- Strike the ball as close to the centre of the court as possible, so that it hits the front wall left of centre and above the cut line.
- Aim to bring the ball back close to the opposite side wall to a good length.

Position when waiting to receive serve.

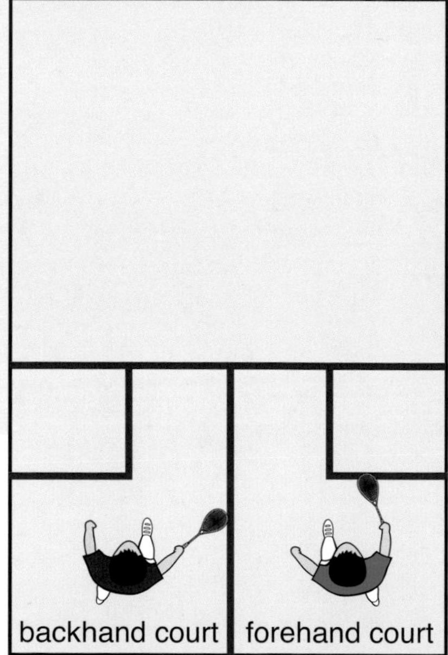

RETURN OF SERVE

To have the best possible chance of returning serve, the receiver must be in position in the opposite back half of the court.

- There are no rules governing where the receiver should stand, but the best position is somewhere in the area shown in the diagram below left.
- This exact position depends on the height and reach of the receiver.

THE RIGHT SPOT

The service receiver should be in a position so that turning and taking one step allows each of the following:

- reaching the back wall with the racket
- a step forward to volley the service
- stepping back to return a serve that is played at the body or down the middle of the court.

The ideal position is somewhere close to the back corners of the service box, clear of the side and back walls.

▼ Notice the position of the player waiting to receive the serve. Always play a backhand shot off the serve to the backhand court, and a forehand shot off the serve to the forehand court (see diagram below left).

VOLLEYED RETURNS

If you feel that your opponent's service is going to fall to a good length, it is best to volley the return. The volley is the best shot to use when returning most serves.

When volleying, try to avoid the following:

- hitting the ball too hard – 'push' the racket face through the ball
- hitting the ball in a downwards direction, unless it is a poor-quality service, which you can attack.

RETURN PRACTICE

Practise a slow high-length return over the server's head as he or she stands in the centre court position. Your practice partner or feeder can play a volley just above the tin in the front corner near to him.

Volley service returns as much as you can.

DEFENDING A GOOD SERVE

The following shots are the best defensive returns of a good service:

- a straight return to a length along the side wall
- a cross-court return to a length. Try to play the ball over your opponent's head to avoid presenting him or her with an easy volley. This return is a risky option because a good volleyer can kill an inaccurate shot with a volley just above the tin.

EQUALITY IN SQUASH

Former England squash international Rebecca Macree was born deaf. She competed at the highest level, representing England in the World and European Team Championships, and reached as high as seventh in the women's world rankings.

Andrew Shelley, Executive Director of the Women's International Squash Players' Association, says, 'Rebecca's long and successful career has been based around great athleticism and drive. She has always hit the ball as sweetly as anybody in the sport. More than this, of course, she has overcome the difficulties posed by deafness to a degree that has been inspirational.'

PLAY DELAYS

Play can be delayed for several reasons.

- Bad light or other circumstances beyond the players' control may stop play.
- If play is resumed the same day, the match continues with the score as it was when play stopped.
- If play is resumed the next or a subsequent day, the score stands unless both players agree to re-start the match.

Rebecca Macree in action.

DROP SHOTS AND ANGLE SHOTS

Drop shots and angle shots need plenty of practice. Once you have mastered these attacking shots, you can use them to score winners. Alternatively, you can use them to incorporate excellent tactics into your game. These shots will move your opponent around the court, making them change direction and forcing errors. You need to practise these as much as your basic drives.

DROP SHOT

There are three different types of drop shot that you can choose to play:

- straight
- angled (commonly used by top professionals)
- cross-court.

There are several different techniques for hitting drop shots. They can be 'cut' or 'pushed', depending on your skill and your intended effect on the ball.

- Keep the racket face open.
- It is necessary to take a shorter backswing and take the ball early by reaching forward with your racket head.
- If you intend to cut the ball, a small amount of backswing is necessary to give the racket head some momentum as it cuts across the inside of the ball. Keep the wrist controlled so that the racket head follows the path of the swing.

TIMING

Top players use the bounce of the ball to their advantage.

- Many players strike the ball very late, well after it has reached the top of its bounce. Good players can choose to strike the ball a few centimetres from the ground.
- In rallies, top players often take the ball early, before the top of its bounce. This speeds up the game, keeping opponents on the move tiring them out.

You should aim for the front wall then the floor near to the side with your drop shot. A ball landing in this area will sit very closely to the side wall and present a difficult shot to play.

DROP SHOT TIPS

Take the ball on the rise or at the top of its bounce.

- Place your leading foot well forward in preparation to play the drop.
- Always adopt a low striking position for drop shots.
- Remember to push back with your leading leg after you have played the drop so that you clear your opponent's path to the ball and recover to the 'T' zone (see page 34) as quickly as possible.

Try to play the ball with touch and correct pace. The correct grip will always produce better drop shots.

POSITIONING FOR THE DROP SHOT

The best positions from which to play the drop shot are shown in the diagram below.

- The most effective positions are in front of the 'T', or centre of the court.
- Shots from further back may succeed against a slow opponent or one who watches the front wall instead of the ball.

When a drop shot is played from the front of the court, push back off your leading foot after playing the shot to recover early back to the 'T' zone, and to give your opponent a clear path to the ball.

The best positions from which to play the drop shot:
A) straight drop shot (target area in red; area from which shot should be played in blue)
B) angled drop shots
C) cross-court drop shot.

PRACTISING THE DROP SHOT

- The best method of practising the drop shot is to start close to the front wall near the centre of the court.
- Tap the ball gently on to the front wall, position yourself for the stroke and play it into one of the front corners.
- Make sure you are happy with your footwork and that you are striking the ball correctly, both early and late. Now move further back in the court until you can play the stroke on to the front wall low down and softly from a position level with the service boxes.

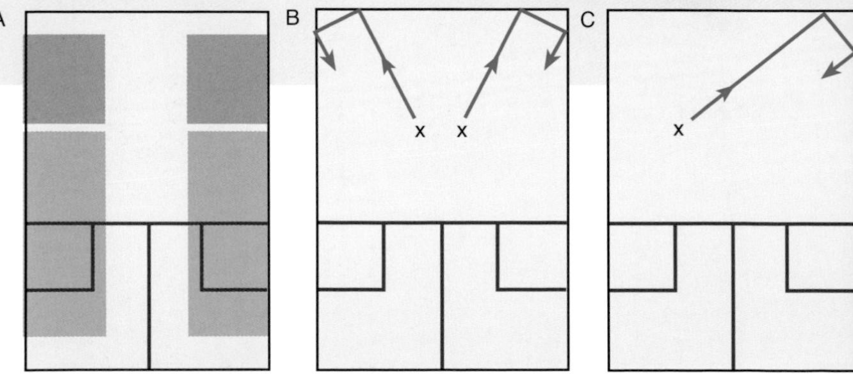

Do not play a drop shot unless your opponent is behind you. He or she must be further back in the court than you are when you strike the ball except for the surprise drop shot from the back of the court off a bad-length shot.

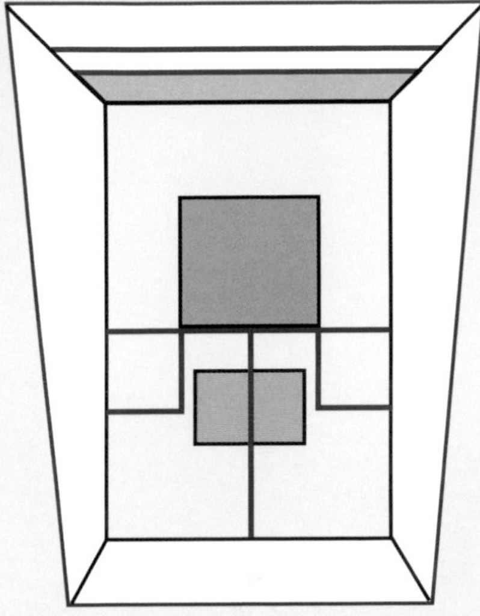

When the ball is dropping in the red sector, your opponent will usually be somewhere in the blue sector – play a drop shot.

DISGUISING THE DROP

- Prepare your racket early before playing the drop shot.
- This causes doubt in the mind of an opponent, who may be expecting you to hit the ball hard to the back of the court.

You can hit the ball hard to the back of the court at the last moment if you hear your opponent moving up the court in anticipation of a drop shot.

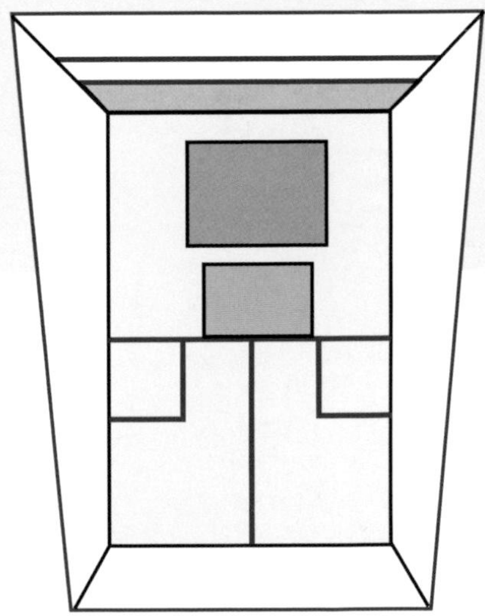

When the ball is dropping further up the court (red sector) your opponent will usually be in the blue sector – play a hard-hit drive to the back of the court.

An angle shot.

DROP SHOT TACTICS

You can usually tell when your opponent is about to play a drop shot, as he or she generally places one foot well forward and crouches a little. Similarly, your opponent will often know when you are going to play a drop shot. It is likely that your opponent will be able to reach your drop, except when you play the perfect stroke.

Use the following tactics to turn your drop shots into winners.

Tactic 1

- Play a number of drops, and you will find that every time you gain a position in front of your opponent, he or she will expect you to play another drop.
- You will have enticed the opponent up the court, close behind you as you play the stroke.
- With a full backswing of the racket, you can either hit the ball hard to the back of the court or lob it gently to the back of the court.

Tactic 2

- Keep very upright as you approach the ball, making it appear that you are going to hit the ball to the back of the court.
- At the last second, bend down or crouch and play a drop shot.
- This is a very difficult shot and needs perfect timing and a great deal of practice.

ANGLE SHOT

The angle shot first hits the side wall, then the front wall and lands near the opposite side wall.
In most cases the shot should be played to change direction of your play and force your opponent to move around the court.

- When you strike the ball on the forehand, the left foot needs to be placed well forward and the left shoulder is well round towards the side wall.
- Similarly, when you strike the ball on the backhand, the right foot is well forward and the right shoulder is well round, pointing at the side wall.

POSITIONING FOR THE ANGLE SHOT

Angle shots can be played from certain positions in the front or back of the court.

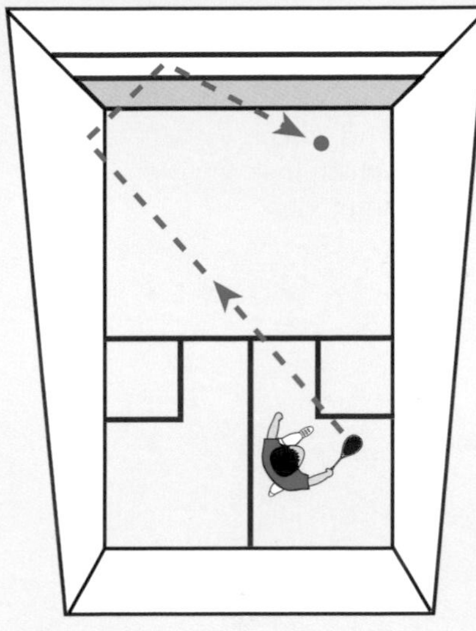

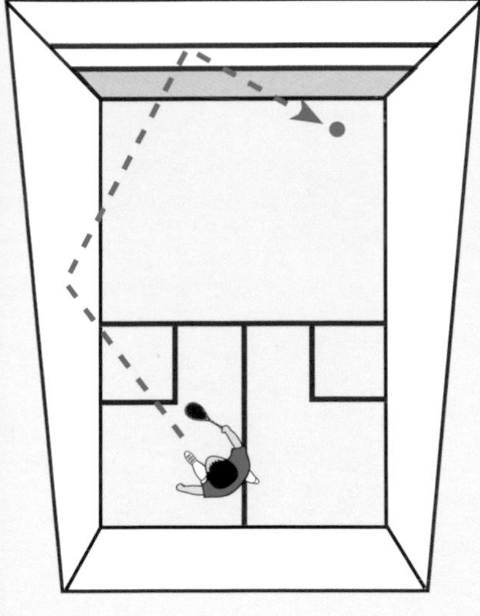

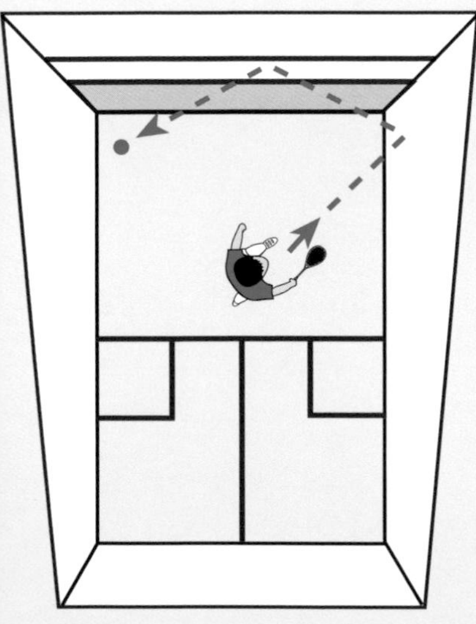

▲ Angle shot played from deep in the court (forehand).

◀ Angle shot played from deep back in the court (backhand).

◀ An angle shot played from in front of the centre line.

It is exhausting to change direction when moving up and down the court. It is far less tiring to run from side to side.

ANGLE SHOT TIPS

- Play an attacking angle shot when your opponent is either behind you or not watching (catching them on the wrong foot).
- Play a defensive angle shot (usually from back of court) when you are under pressure and have no alternative.

ANGLE SHOT TACTICS

Disguising your strokes is very important in squash. A player often has to play a stroke on the forehand from a position fairly far back in the court. Disguise your angle shots by using the following tactics.

Tactic 1
The position in the court and the stroke for tactic 1 are shown in the diagram.

- The usual stroke in this case is to hit the ball up the forehand side wall and back into the back corner.
- By placing your shoulder further round towards the side wall and making a full swing of the racket, you can take the ball late and play an angle shot.
- You must hit the ball hard and play it late.

Tactic 1: a disguised angle shot played late. The player's position and direction means this shot must be played hard and late.

Equally effective is the same stoke played from deep back in the court on the backhand.

Tactic 2
Tactic 2 is very similar, but the strokes are played in the front of the court.

- During a rally, you will often find yourself playing a stroke well up the court on the forehand.
- From this position, you usually play either a drop shot or hit the ball hard to the back of the court.
- By placing your left shoulder further round towards the side wall, you can play a quick little angle shot.
- You must take a full swing of the racket and play the ball late.

The same stroke played from well up the court on the backhand is another potential winner.

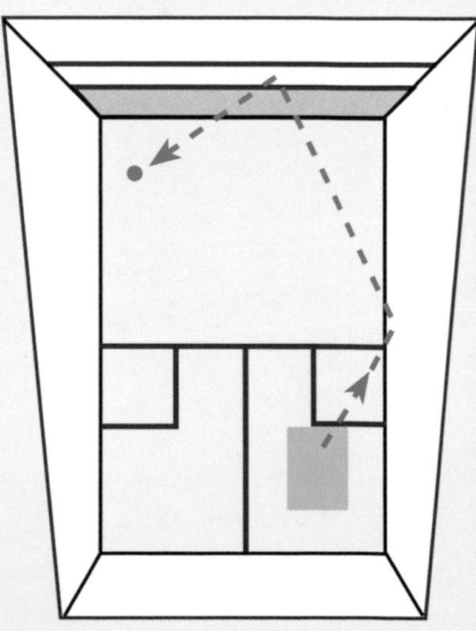

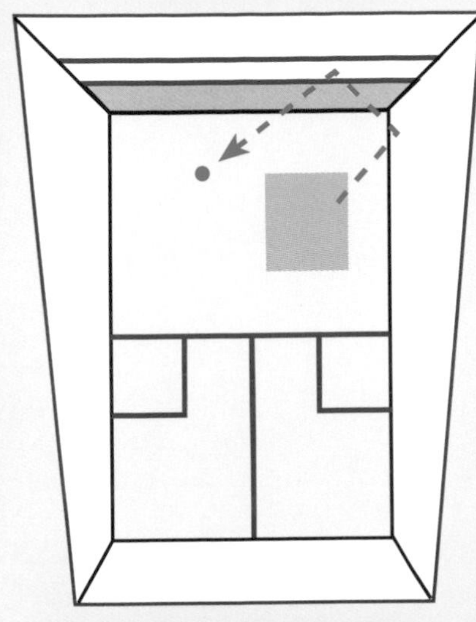

Tactic 2: position for a disguised angle shot played quick and late from the front of the court.

Practise taking angle shots on the rise and early, because this speeds up the game and your opponent is made to move faster up the court.

VOLLEYING AND LOBBING

Volleying and lobbing are difficult strokes to execute but very important shots in the game and potentially deadly winners. The lob can be used in both attack and defence. Top players try to volley as much as they can, and you can learn a lot about when to volley and lob, and from what position, by watching competitive games and better players. It is crucial to include these two shots in all your game plans.

VOLLEYING

Most of the top players look to volley the ball as much as possible because this has the effect of speeding up the game, pressurising your opponent's movement and allowing you to keep a good position in middle of court.

- If you are going to volley, it is important to keep the racket up at all times since this reduces the amount of time needed to hit the ball.
- Players who dangle or trail their racket tend not to be instinctive volleyers.

One of the most important volleys is the return of a good service. Do not allow the ball into the back corner, and follow the principles mentioned in the earlier section on service returns.

VOLLEYING PRACTICE

- Take up a position in the centre of the court.
- From the wall, feed yourself balls between waist- and head-height at different distances from the wall.
- Volley each ball either short into the front two corners, or deep into the back two corners.

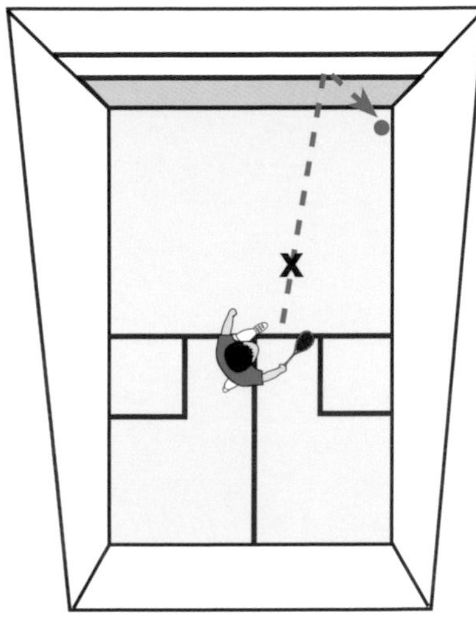

Volleys from the middle of the court. Players with fast reactions and good movement can intercept poor cross-court shots from as far forward as the point marked with a cross, putting pressure on the opponent.

WHEN TO VOLLEY

Learn to look for volleys from across the middle of the court. You have two choices of target from here:

1. Volleying deep, which buries the opponent in the back corners.
2. Taking the ball short and low into the two front corners. This option is more risky because the ball is being taken low on to the front wall, but if played correctly this shot can be a rally winner.

These strokes are best played when your opponent is well out of position behind you.

If you play against a person who trails their racket, you should occasionally hit the ball hard down the centre of the court, i.e. at the player standing in the centre of the court.

LOBBING

The lob can be one of the most important strokes in the game, either in defence or attack. It is fair to say it is the most under-used shot at all levels.

- In defence it enables the striker to return to a position on the 'T' before an opponent can play a stroke.
- In attack it can be devastating when played accurately and to length, especially on a cold court.
- A good lob serve can immediately put you into an attacking position in a rally.

A lob can be a good option in attack or defence.

DOUBLES

Squash doubles involves two teams of two playing against each other on the same court. Doubles courts are the same length as singles courts but are 1.2m wider; however, doubles games are often played on singles courts.

In essence, the game is the same as singles. However, each pairing plays alternate strokes with the opposition. There is no requirement for the pair to alternate with each other, as they would in table tennis for example.

While there are a few variations on singles squash – notably the scoring, which is a point-a-rally up to 15 – the only other major difference is a rule by which many points are played as lets. This is primarily for safety reasons – with four players swinging rackets in a small space, it is important to minimise the risk of players hitting each other.

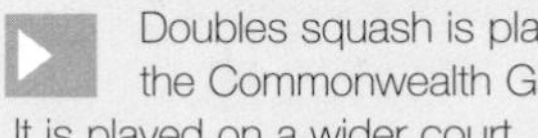
Doubles squash is played at the Commonwealth Games. It is played on a wider court.

LOBBING TIPS

- The ball can be lobbed from any of the four corners of the court.
- A good target is to get the ball out of your opponent's reach when on the 'T'.
- The ball will usually hit high on the front wall. The only exception to this will be when the player is attempting a lob from a position close to the front wall.
- The ball must pass over your opponent's head as he or she stands in the court.
- The lob is best played across the court, and should strike the side wall and bounce on the floor to behind the service box. This type of lob makes your opponent play a defensive return because it is very risky to play a smash. If he or she lets it drop in the back corners it should be 'dying'.

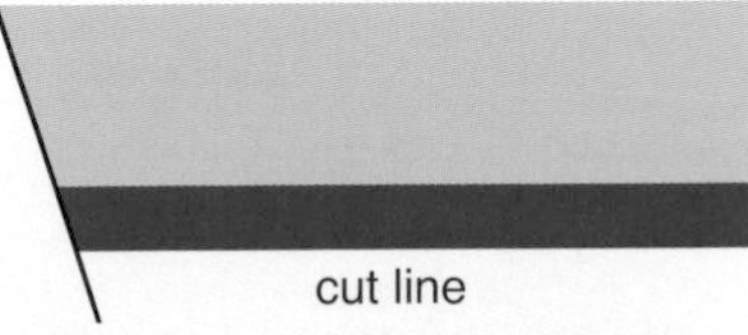

The blue area indicates where the lob shot usually hits the front wall.

GAME ON

Squash is an 'open skill' sport. Every time the ball is played, the environment changes: if a ball bounces in a different place, you change your position and footwork each time, for example. Compare this to a 'closed skill' sport, such as discus throwing, where everything is predictable with a clear beginning and end.

LEARNING OPEN SKILLS

The challenge for new squash players is to learn to play the game in this 'open skill' context. They must learn how to develop their perception skills so that they can build rallies well and apply simple, effective tactics. These are the skills of squash.

'T' TO 'T' SQUASH

Perception skills are used in this simple process. Repeat the following sequence for every shot you play.

From the 'T' zone, you must try to:

- **read** the shot your opponent is going to play (watch the opponent's body, racket and ball), then move early into a position where you want to play the ball
- **decide** which shot you want to play
- **play** the shot.

Try to read your opponent's shots, and always watch the ball.

Improve the accuracy of your shots by hitting different shots to specific targets set down on the court.

Having done this, you must recover back to the 'T' zone as quickly as possible.

CHOOSING YOUR SHOT

During the 'decide' phase, it is important to choose the correct shot at the correct time. Follow this simple what, why, when, how method:

- **what** do you want the ball to do?
- **why** do you want to play that shot?
- **when** should you play that shot in a rally?
- **how** do you play the shot?

Practise this process and you will quickly develop better tactical knowledge, and understand exactly how to play 'open skill' squash.

TACTICAL PRINCIPLES OF SQUASH

Following these simple principles will help you to choose your shots well and play the game in a more intelligent way.

1. Hit the ball to good target areas
You must practise your technique and develop good ball control to enable you to play the ball accurately. Squash is a positional game: the more accurate your shots, the better the positions you can take up.

Learning when to attack and when to defend helps players to build successful rallies.

TACTICAL PRINCIPLES (continued)

2. Play the right shot at the right time
Use the 'what?, why?, when?, how?' method for each shot, to practise playing the correct shot for the situation. You will quickly understand when you are playing rallies in the best way. You will also see that playing the right shot allows you to stay in control of the rally and therefore have the best chance of winning it!

3. Attack and defend at the right times
The best players make remarkably few mistakes. They play accurate shots to all areas of the court, and create time for themselves on court. They know that with fast, economical movement, good perception skills and awareness of what is happening on court, it is possible to return almost everything, either in a defensive or attacking way.

- An attacking shot – could be a volley to length, a drop shot or angle shot, which causes your opponent to move under pressure on to the ball.
- A defensive shot – could be a drive played high on the front wall, or a lob played softly: both shots give you time to recover back to the 'T' zone.

Moving quickly to the ball and then back to the 'T' zone once the shot has been played gives the best chance of controlling the game.

Try to keep the ball out of the danger area (see page 47).

4. Building rallies (playing four corners)
Your aim should be to build rallies, which creates chances to win points, games and matches. Do not be in a hurry to attempt a winning shot. You need to use your drive and volley to consistently put your opponent under pressure in the back corners. You can then control the 'T' zone and be in a position to attack with a volley drop, drop shot or angle shot, or another shot that may win the rally.

- You need to play to all four corners of the court in order to win rallies.
- Change the pace of your play, to break up the rhythm of your opponent's games and maintain control of play.
- A common error is not experimenting with the height of the front wall. You can play at different pace either above or below the cut line.
- Experiment with your game and your tactics. Prepare game plans around your strengths.

Defensive play aims to buy time in a rally, to let you recover your 'T' zone position.

THE DANGER AREA

The danger area is across the middle part of the court in which, if you leave the ball, you can expect an attacking shot from your opponent.

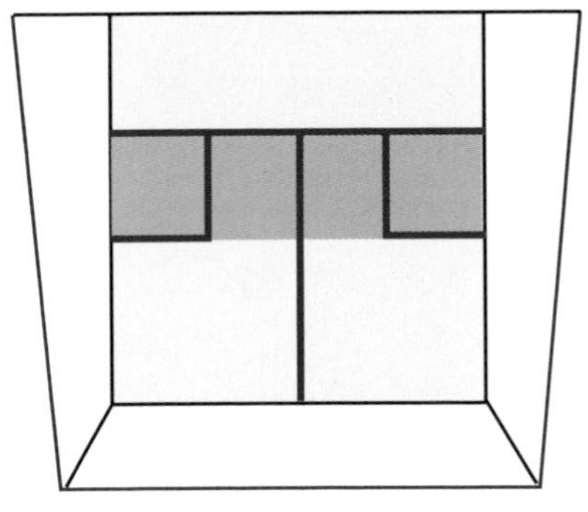

The danger area: the opponent can take the ball into the front of the court – either directly with effective drop shots or with side wall shots. He or she can increase pressure by playing hard cross-court shots or straight lengths.

SOLO PRACTICE

If you find yourself on court alone, either because your opponent has not turned up or because you have arrived early, what can you do that will improve your game? Do you just knock the ball up and down the wall until you are bored enough to stop, or do you need a set pattern to work to?

WORK OUT

Solo practice is far from boring if you have a constructive pattern in mind. It can be really hard work depending on how much effort you put in. Many club players would probably not choose to practise alone, but for the top professionals solo practice is a very important part of their squash schedule.

Solo practice makes more sense if the session is divided into phases. The following section describes a series of practices in four distinct phases that will take you through a 30–40 minute solo training session. It starts with a warm-up and ends with a series of difficult strokes.

PHASE 1

Warm up properly with some stretches and then build up body heat with some slow all-court 'ghosting' (simulating squash movements with no ball) for 2 or 3 minutes.

PHASE 2

Now that you are warm you must get the ball warm. On your forehand side choose one of these target areas:

- between the side wall and the outside line of the service box (the tramline)
- anywhere within the forehand side of the court.

Choose your target area according to your playing standard.

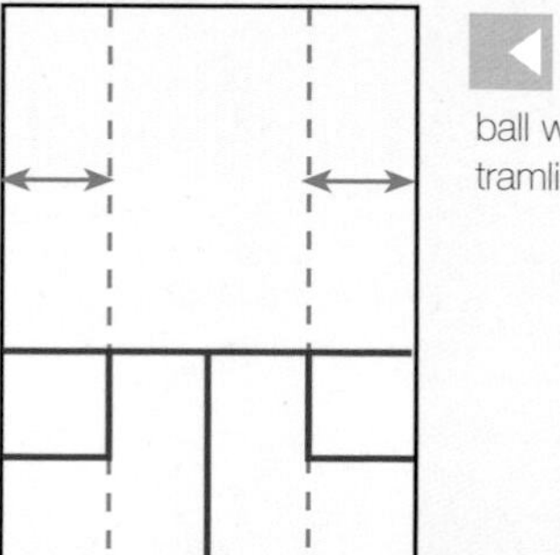

Phase 2: keep the ball within the tramlines.

Keeping strictly on the forehand, try hitting this target area 50 times consecutively without a mistake. If you hit the ball off course or on the backhand, start again from scratch until you achieve your goal. Set your own number, making sure that it is realistic but challenging.

If you have pretty good ball control, when you make a mistake, recover the ball to the target area before it bounces more than twice. This keeps the ball in continuous play and makes you work harder.

Once you have achieved your target on the forehand, repeat the exercise on the backhand. Alter the target area or the number of consecutive hits, depending on which is your stronger side.

After warming up, you will probably find that you are more alert and ready to practise hard.

PHASE 3

This phase of the training session will help to improve your ball control.

Target practice

Select a target area anywhere in the service box. Beginning on your forehand, hit the ball so that it lands in the target area a pre-set number of times, for example between 5 and 15.

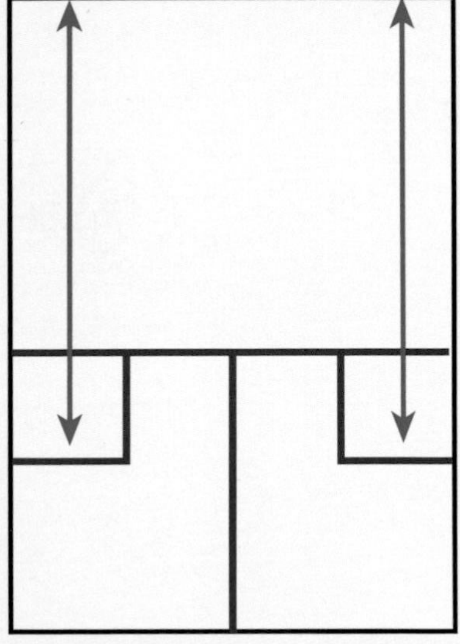

Phase 3 target practice: the service boxes are the target.

If you hit too short or too long, do not stop – correct the length, sticking to the one-bounce rule, and start from scratch until the number of consecutive hits is achieved. As before, repeat on the other side.

Length to length

Hit the ball to such a length down the side wall that it bounces once on to the back wall and is then returned to do the same again.

- This exercise requires excellent timing of the swing in the back of the court. It also involves good use of the face of the racket in order to get under the ball to lift it high (above the cut line) on to the front wall so that it returns to a good length.
- Once again, set yourself a target number – between 3 and 30 for example, depending on your standard. For your first few attempts, set a low target because it is difficult to repeat this shot successfully early on.
- Try to correct any mistakes without stopping, even if it means playing a boast and then retrieving to the practice area.
- When you have completed the forehand, change to the backhand.

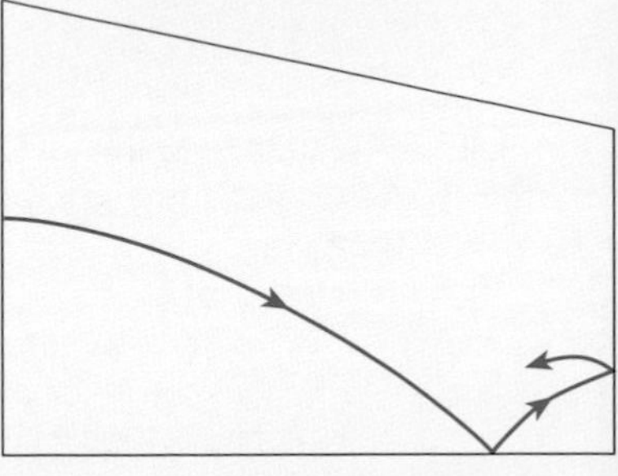

Hitting length to length.

PHASE 4

Now move to the front of the court for phase 4 to complete your solo practice session.

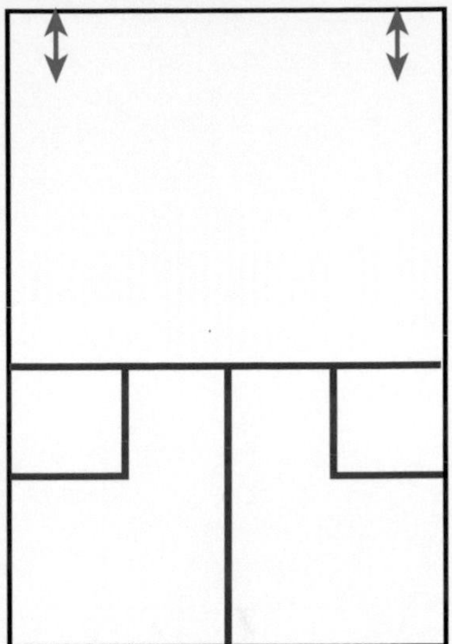

Position yourself about 2m from the front wall to practise short volleys.

Front court volleys

To practise volleys from the front of the court, you will need to position yourself about 2m from the front wall on the forehand side.

- Begin volleying the ball on to the front wall at a reasonably fast rate, attempting to keep the wrist firm and the racket face open to hit slightly underneath the ball.
- Using only a short backswing, punch the ball on to the front wall.
- Now try to keep this going at a good rate for between 10 and 60 consecutive volleys without a mistake.
- Keep the ball in play and change to the backhand.
- If you make a mistake, which is highly likely, only allow the ball to bounce once before retrieving it, and resume counting.
- Still without allowing the ball to hit the floor, move towards one of the front corners and volley on the forehand and backhand around the angle for your set number, making sure that you stand a reasonable distance out and controlling the wrist from forehand to backhand.

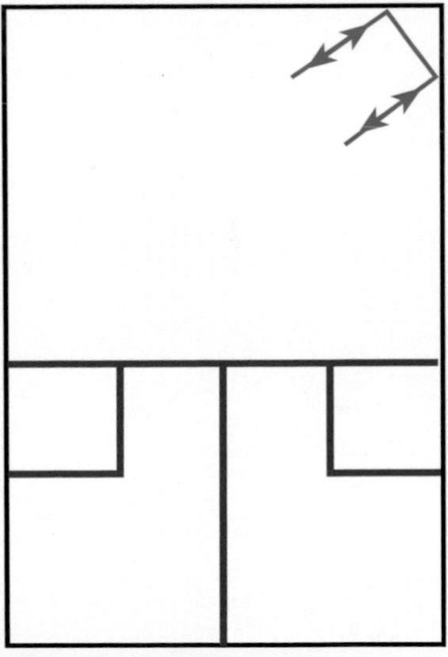

Move to the side wall and continue practising short volleys into the corner.

Drop and angle shots

This is a difficult exercise to keep going because the idea is to practise finishing the rally rather than playing shots that can be returned easily.

- Start off by playing forehand and backhand angle and reverse angle shots across the front of the court, deciding which shot to play as you go.
- Do not allow the ball to bounce more than once, keeping the routine moving from angles to drops.
- Hit both straight angled and cross-court shots off the bounce and on the volley, play the ball to all positions around the front of the court, and then play a drop but try to retrieve it and set yourself up with another from a different position.

If you find yourself with only 10 minutes to spare, attempt only one of the practices.

SETTING YOUR TARGETS

Set a time limit for drop and angle shot practice, for example 4 minutes.

- Count how many errors you make.
- More than two mistakes per minute is too many, so over a period of 4 minutes try to make no more than eight mistakes.
- Do not count a winning shot as a mistake if you are unable to retrieve it – mistakes are balls that end up in the tin.

Combos

To finish, try a combination of shots on the volley if you feel you are good enough, or alternatively off the bounce.

- Start close to the front wall on the forehand side and, over 20 strokes, lengthen the hit until you have moved back past the short line, keeping the ball under control.
- When you have achieved 20 consecutive shots without stopping, change to the backhand and gradually move forwards until you are once again close to the front wall after another 20 shots.

- Keeping the ball in play, move to the centre of the front wall and play 20 forehand to backhand angles across the body.
- Finally, try 20 figure-of-eight shots, i.e. forehand across the body to hit the front wall, side wall and return across the body to hit the opposite corner, front wall and side wall.

By the time you have completed the final phase of this practice session, if you have set reasonable targets, you will have been on court for about 30–40 minutes.

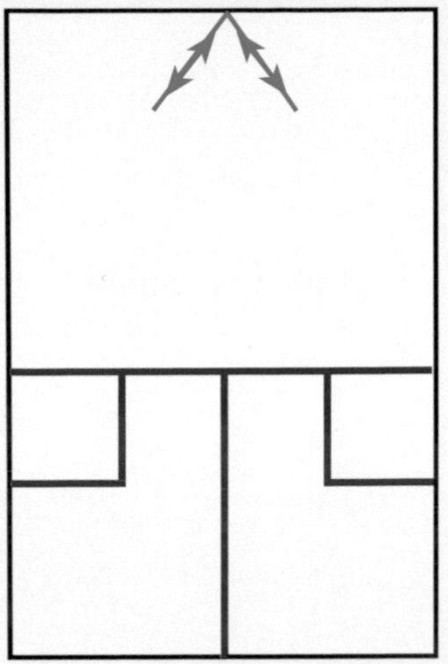

Move to the centre of the front wall and play 20 forehand to backhand angles across the body.

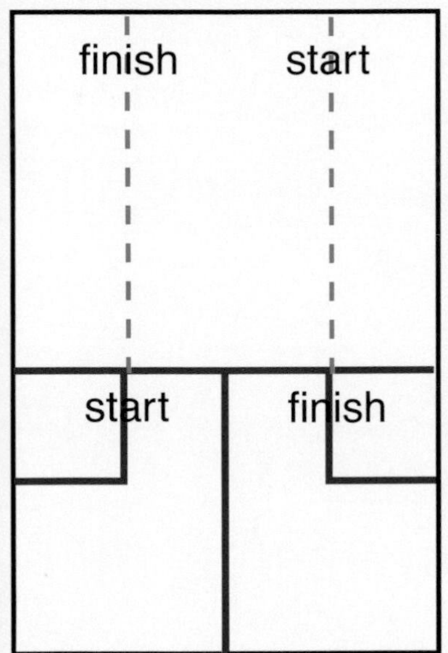

Phase 4 combination shots: up and down. Start close to the wall and play 20 volleyed strokes, moving past to the short line.

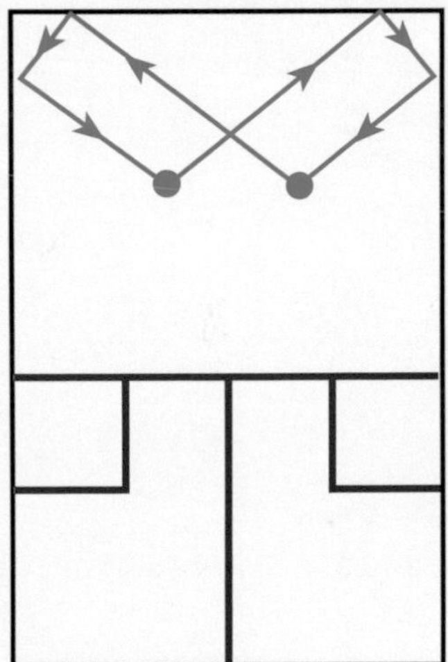

Phase 4 figure-of-eight shots. These are played forehand across the body to hit the front wall and side wall. The return is played across the body to hit the opposite corner, front wall and side wall.

RACKETBALL

Racketball is an alternative game to squash, played on the same courts and with similar rules. It is easier than squash, with a larger ball and shorter racket. Racketball can be a useful introduction to a squash-like game, as well as being a game in its own right.

THE COURT

Racketball is played on a squash court. All the markings are the same, except that:

- the front-wall service line is not used
- the ball must hit the front wall between the out-of-court line at the top of the front wall and the tin at the bottom.

RACKETS

Racketball rackets are shorter than those used for squash. They are not allowed to be longer than 56cm, including any bumper strip. Rackets must have a head no wider than 28cm, and weigh no more than 250g. The frame can be made of any material, though most are carbon fibre or alloy.

There are several other rules to do with the racket:

- a thong can be used to attach the handle to the player's wrist
- strings must be recessed in the racket head, or protected by a bumper strip. The bumper strip must be non-marking and made of a soft material
- strings must be of gut, nylon or a substitute material, but must not be metal.

In the USA, racketball (or racquetball, as it is known there) is played on a court measuring 40 ft long x 20 ft wide x 20 ft high (12.2m x 6.1m x 6.1m).

BALLS

The balls used in racketball are larger than for squash, and bounce more freely. They do not need to be 'warmed up' before reaching their full potential, as squash balls do. Racketball balls weigh between 39g and 41g, and have a diameter of 53–57mm, about the same as a tennis ball without its cloth covering.

'Recreational' balls are the easiest to play with, as they are more bouncy. They are coloured blue, and bounce to 112–114cm when dropped from a height of 254cm in a temperature of 25°C.

'Competition' balls are coloured black, and are less bouncy than recreational balls. They bounce to 88–90cm when dropped from a height of 254cm in a temperature of 25°C.

A YOUNG SPORT

Racketball is a relatively new sport, which was invented in the UK.

- It only formally became a sport for the first time in 1984.
- It was invented by Ian Wright, a squash player and referee.

Racketball equipment is slightly smaller than that of squash.

SCORING

Players score a point when their opponent fails to return the ball. The receiver can also win a point if the server serves a double fault.

Racketball is usually the best of either three or five games. Each game is won when one of the players reaches 15 points. If both players reach 14 points, the winner is the first to reach 17. The exception is in the last (i.e. third or fifth game), where the game is won when one player gets 2 points clear. So, for example, a score of 13-15, 17-15, 24-26 would be possible.

SERVING

The server must have at least part of one foot touching the floor inside the service box. Before it is hit, the ball is bounced on the floor (but it must not touch the wall). The server hits the ball straight to the front wall, aiming to hit it between the tin at the bottom and the out-of-court line at the top.

The served ball must also be hit in such a way that it will fall into the opposite rear quarter of the court. It can touch a side wall on its way, but it must not hit the back wall without first bouncing on the floor.

SERVICE FAULTS

Players can make a single service fault and get a second chance to serve. Two service faults will hand the service to their opponent. Single service faults are as follows:

- the ball is not bounced before it is served
- the served ball hits the back wall before it has hit the floor.

Servers can also lose the point straight away if they make the following mistakes:

- the ball touches the wall before being served, the server fails to hit it after it has bounced, or the server hits it more than once
- the served ball hits the back wall outside the correct area, or hits any other part of the court before it hits the correct area.

TACTICAL TIPS

- **The basic idea of racketball is to hit the ball as far from your opponent as possible, making it harder to return. Sometimes this requires a hard shot; sometimes a softer, short ball will be better.**
- **After hitting the ball, try to get back to a position near where the short line and the mid-court line meet. This lets you cover the whole court for your next shot.**

CHANGE OF SERVE

Service changes depending on who has won the last point. Whoever won the point serves for the next one. So if the server loses the point, he or she hands the right to serve to their opponent.

If the served ball hits the corner of the back wall and floor, it is a good serve.

Racketball is an exciting, fast-moving game.

SQUASH AND RACKETBALL CHRONOLOGY

Squash rackets is a ball game very like rackets, from which it was developed. The main differences are that squash rackets – usually called squash – is played in a smaller court, using a somewhat shorter racket and a hollow ball of black or coloured composition.

1890 The first reference to the game of squash rackets appeared in the *Badminton Library of Sports and Pastimes*. The soft ball was introduced at Harrow School, in England, as a basis for learning to play tennis and rackets. There was no standardisation of courts.

1901 Eustace Miles, World Champion rackets and tennis player, wrote the first book on the game of squash. He stated that the game was played and enjoyed by thousands in various parts of the world, although only in England was the game included in school and university activities.

1907 The first recognised championship of any country was held. John A. Miskey of Philadelphia won the American National.

1920 The first Professional Championship of the British Isles was played between the only two entrants, Charles R. Read and Ariel W.B. Johnson. The next championship, between the same players, did not take place until 1928 when the results were repeated.

1921 A woman became the first British Amateur Champion of either sex, when Mrs Joyce Cave won the title, one year before the men. A '15-up' scoring system continued until 1926 when the '9-point' system was adopted.

1924 Charles Arnold, the Bath Club (London) professional, wrote the first English coaching manual. It included the first set of rules on the 'soft-ball' version of squash rackets, produced by the Tennis and Rackets Association.

1928 The English Squash Rackets Association was founded to act as the central authority and to formulate, add to and alter the rules governing the game.

1931 Egypt, Australia and New Zealand had formed organising bodies. The great Egyptian player F.D. Amr Bey won the first of his five British Open Championships in 1932. He retired undefeated in 1937.

1950 A report from the newly founded Pakistan Squash Rackets Association mentioned a player destined to change the history of the game. This 'tough young player' was Hashim Khan.

1951 On his first visit to Britain, Hashim Khan won every match and this continued until 1956. He won the British Open final to become unofficial World Champion at his first attempt, without the loss of a game. This was a truly remarkable performance for a man nearly 35 years of age.

1967 The International Squash Rackets Federation was founded. The founder members were Australia, Egypt, Great Britain, India, New Zealand, Pakistan and South Africa. The World Championships were inaugurated for individuals and teams. Jonah Barrington won the British Open; he was to win again in 1968, 1970, 1971, 1972 and finally in 1973.

1973 Problems with amateur status in sport resulted in the game going Open (professional). Regional Associations were being formed, and the European Squash Rackets Federation was founded in 1973, followed by the Asian and others.

1976 The Women's International Squash Rackets Federation was formed. Geoff Hunt of Australia won the first men's World Open Championship. Australia's Heather McKay won the first women's World Open Championship.

1977 Heather McKay of Australia won her sixteenth consecutive British Open women's title.

1982–1991 Pakistan dominated the championships for men, with Jahangir Khan winning the British Open for ten consecutive years. Jansher Khan then won every Open until 1995.

1998 Squash is included in the Commonwealth Games in Kuala Lumpur, Malaysia.

GLOSSARY

Angle shot A shot played at an angle to change the direction of play and force your opponent to move around the court.

Backswing Preparation of the stroke. The height of backswing varies depending on the type of shot that you wish to play.

Behind the leading foot (taking the ball late) Hitting the ball when it has passed your front foot, a position that is usually used when you need to hit the side walls before the front wall.

Boast A common return from the back corners, hitting under the ball, and lifting it upwards on to the side wall, making an angle that will carry the ball from the side wall on to the front wall in the opposite front corner.

Cutting the ball Putting spin on the ball using the racket face.

Danger area The middle part of the court. Leave the ball here and expect an attacking shot from your opponent!

Down A service that is not below the service line or to the floor.

Fault A playing error that results in the right to serve being lost.

Follow-through The final phase of a stroke.

Foot fault A service fault due to the server not having at least one foot in contact with the service box when striking the ball.

Grip The technique used to hold the racket.

Hand-in The player serving to start a rally.

Hand-out The player receiving the serve.

Leading foot The foot that is closest to the ball prior to striking.

Length to length Hitting the ball to such a length down the side wall that it bounces on to the back wall and returns.

Let An undecided rally. The rally does not score and the server serves again from the same box.

Lob A shot that, in defence, enables the striker to return to a position on the 'T' before an opponent can play a stroke and, in attack, can be devastating.

Marker The person who calls the play and the score.

Not up Describes a service that is hit incorrectly.

On the fall (also called 'late') Describes the ball after it has reached its apex. A strike used out of necessity, or when getting your opponent to commit to a shot where he or she then has to change direction to cover another shot.

On the rise (also called 'early') Describes the ball before it reaches its apex, the highest point the ball reaches after it has bounced, before it then drops off the bounce towards the floor.

PAR (point-a-rally) system Refers to scoring system used in the men's professional game, where games are up to 11 points and every point is scored.

Racketball A similar game to squash, played on the same courts but with a larger ball and shorter racket.

Rally A continuous sequence of shots played alternately by each player.

Set one Indicates that the game in progress is to be played to 9 points after the score has reached 8-all.

Set two Indicates that the game in progress is to be played to 10 points after the score has reached 8-all.

Shot positioning The position you take up before you strike the ball.

Standard (or International) system Refers to the scoring system used in the women's professional game, where games are up to 9 points and points can only be scored when you are serving hand-in.

Strike The part of the stroke when the racket face makes contact with the ball.

'T' zone The area marked by the 'T' shape in the centre of the court floor.

Taking the ball on the rise Hitting the ball before it has reached its apex. This allows players to speed up the game by taking the ball early and hurrying their opponent.

Tin The out-of-court area situated at the bottom of the front wall.

Top of the bounce The apex, or highest point, in a ball's path after it has bounced. At this point the ball is moving at its slowest and is easiest to hit.

Tramline The outside line of the service box.

INDEX